Lisa
Freeman

Scholastic

SCHOLASTIC BOOK SERVICES
New York Toronto London Auckland Sydney Tokyo

ISBN 0-590-31787-3

Copyright © 1980 by Scholastic Magazines, Inc. All rights reserved. Published by Scholastic Book Services, a Division of Scholastic Magazines, Inc.

12 11 10 9 8 7 6 5 4 3 2 1   11   0 1 2 3 4 5/8

Printed in the U.S.A.   01

SHAUN CASSIDY:
Back with Breaking Away

"After the Hardy Boys, I had had it with television," reflects 22-year-old Shaun as he puts Roquefort dressing on his salad at the 20th Century-Fox commissary. "I was thrilled when I got the part, but what I really wanted to do was make records. My schedule on that show was so tight I used to be at the studio still filming at nine at night. After that I would go to the recording studio until midnight or later, and I still had to be back to film by ten the next morning."

But now Shaun's found a new television series to star in and feels enough excitement about doing it that he's willing to put off recording for a while. Its a spinoff of the Oscar-nominated motion picture *Breaking Away,* which delighted millions with the antics of four high school buddies in the small college town of Bloomington, Indiana. This season their adventures will continue each week on ABC-TV.

The guys are devoted to one another and dedicated to creating a lot of mischief for the university students, who ridicule them for their small-town ways.

Shaun enjoys his role as Dave, whose constant sunny view of life is similar to his. "I've always been an optimistic person," says Shaun, and even his wife, actress and model Ann Pennington, claims he's a very positive person.

"He's also really considerate and kind," she adds. "He tries to make everyone feel young and happy."

It wasn't hard for Shaun to learn his role as Dave. "When I first saw the script for the show

2

I knew right away I wanted to do it. I get to sing Italian songs and speak a little Italian. Even though my character isn't Italian, he's just a little happy-go-lucky and likes the fun he has pretending he's Italian."

Although while he was growing up Shaun rode a bicycle, for his role in *Breaking Away* he had to learn about bike racing. "It's a little different from pleasure riding—even the bicycle is different. You have to pace yourself throughout the race so you'll have a burst of energy for the finish. And there are ways to lean forward to get the most help from the wind."

Since portions of *Breaking Away* will be filmed on location in Georgia where most of the pilot was shot, Shaun may have to have two homes—one in the South for filming season, usually July through February, and one in Hollywood, which he already has.

He lives there with his wife of several months. "A lot of people told me not to get married, that it wouldn't be good for my career," Shaun reflects. "But I knew that if my fans really cared about me and for my personal happiness, they'd wish me all the luck and just be glad for me."

Apparently Shaun was right. Not only have his fans accepted his marriage, but his career is doing better than ever and he's especially pleased with his latest album. "It's different from anything I've ever done before," he proudly proclaims. "I went to New York and recorded it with rock star Todd Rundgren producing. It was a new sound for me and a new direction, and I hope my old fans will like it and that it will attract new fans as well.''

Shaun also has a TV special, which should be aired some time this season. "I guess it depends upon whether or not *Breaking Away* is a success,'' Shaun says. "If the series is popular, they'll want to air the special right away and probably even have me do another one. I guess that's show business for you.''

On *Breaking Away,* Shaun stars with Jackie Earle Haley, who is recreating the role he had in the film. As Moocher, Jackie really goes bananas when anyone calls him Shorty. Maybe you remember him from his role in the movie *The Bad News Bears*, in which he played the outfielder.

Brawny Mike is played by Tom Wiggins, and Tom Bray plays Cyril, the sardonic, funny guy, with Vincent Gardenia and Barbara Barrie rounding out the cast as Dave's parents. Barbara Barrie is also recreating her film role, but all the other characters have been newly cast for TV.

"It's a wonderful group to work with,'' Shaun says, putting down his fork and getting ready to head back to the set. "I think we've got good scripts, a talented cast, and a good crew backing us up. I feel pleased with the quality of the product and I hope the audience feels the same way. After all, it doesn't matter how good you think you are. If nobody's watching your show you're not going to make it.''

Hopefully, Shaun's series will be a success for him. With all the hard work, energy, and love he puts into it—it should be!

THOSE AMAZING ANIMALS REALLY ARE!

Most people don't like spiders in their house, or crawling on their arm, and they wouldn't want to come face to face with a shark. But everyone is interested in learning about animals, seeing how they live and survive—from a distance!

That's what makes *Those Amazing Animals* so amazing. The cameras have captured the incredible but true happenings of the wondrous and amazing animal kingdom — from the surprising crying frog, to a queen termite in Africa that has laid 10,000 eggs a day for 50 years, to a dog that cries and a rooster that laughs. It all sounds amazing, but it's just a sample of what *Those Amazing Animals* will be bringing you each week.

The one-hour informational series is an intriguing exploration of wild, exotic, dangerous, endangered, and just plain "different" animals. It's the kind of show that holds your attention, and maybe even makes you hold your breath!

Bringing you the fascinating stories each week are the show's hosts, famous actor Burgess Meredith, Priscilla Presley, and Jim Stafford, who, incidentally, rose to fame in 1974 with his hit single, "Spiders and Snakes."

"I guess I fit right in with the theme of the show," laughs Jim, who has a way with people that makes them feel comfortable and easy. That's why he's such a good host for the show. The more he talks the more you want to listen.

Jim was born in Winter Haven, Florida, and first got interested in show business through music. "I picked up my first guitar at the age of fourteen and taught myself how to use it," he admits. He went on to work with a group called The Legends but soon went solo and has been working alone since—until *Those Amazing Animals,* that is. Now he's partnered with lovely Priscilla Presley, who's making her prime-time show business debut on this series!

You probably already know Priscilla is the ex-wife of the late superstar Elvis Presley, and has an almost 12-year-old daughter, Lisa, who is delighted her mom will be working with all those interesting animals.

Priscilla may look brave on the series when she lets tarantulas crawl over her arm, or sits down next to a roaring lion, but she admits it takes a lot of getting used to. "It's always safe, and we've got animal trainers and experts around us all the time, but it still takes a little daring," she smiles. "It's not easy to stick out your hand to a wild animal, or swallow your fears and look a rattlesnake in the eye!"

Of course Jim, Priscilla, and Burgess won't be doing anything dangerous or anything that would hurt them or endanger them in any way, but part of the excitement and interest in learning about these creatures depends upon close contact with some of these animals, who are very, very amazing!

CHARLIE'S ANGELS— PAST AND PRESENT

There has never been a television series like *Charlie's Angels,* a show with a constantly changing cast that doesn't seem to slip in the popularity polls no matter how many angels appear and disappear.

Kate Jackson, Farrah Fawcett-Majors, and Jaclyn Smith started it all in the fall season of 1976. *Charlie's Angels* quickly became one of the top-rated shows, and the Angel's faces appeared on the covers of dozens of magazines all over the world.

One angel in particular seemed to capture the hearts of America: Farrah, the blond, blue-eyed beauty whose wide, flashing smile and feathered mane became her trademark and started a nationwide craze. Girls everywhere tried the "Farrah" look, and her pin-up poster was a top-seller for months. Everywhere Farrah went she was mobbed by adoring fans trying to get close to her. It became impossible for her to go anywhere without a bodyguard.

Alabama-born Kate Jackson was the most experienced actress among the angels. She first became known to audiences in her role as Jill Danko on TV's *The Rookies,* but her popularity soared when she became Sabrina Duncan on *Angels.* In her role, Kate was the "leader" of the three detectives.

Jaclyn Smith stepped into her role as Kelly Garrett from a modeling career. Everyone calls her Jackie, and she was born in Houston, Texas, where she dreamed of becoming a ballet dancer—but decided on an acting career instead.

When the series began, Farrah was the only married angel in real life. The Six Million Dollar

Man, Lee Majors, was her husband of several years, but the two have since separated, and Farrah now goes by the name of Farrah Fawcett. The charismatic star decided to leave *Charlie's Angels* in pursuit of an acting career in 1978, but since she had signed a contract with the show, she had to return for six guest appearances over the next two seasons, which she has since done. If Farrah appears on the show at all this year, it will be as a guest star, and because she wants to.

There was a nationwide search to find an angel to fill Farrah's shoes, and Cheryl Ladd was the lucky lady chosen to play Chris Monroe—sister to Farrah's character, Jill. As Chris, Cheryl was immediately accepted by the TV public and says she loves her role on the series.

The next year it was Kate Jackson who got restless in her angel role and wanted to move on to films and other projects. Kate, who married actor Andrew Stevens shortly after leaving the show, was replaced by Shelly Hack after a long, and heavily promoted, campaign to find a replacement.

Shelly moved into the show in the role of Tiffany Wells, and viewers knew her mostly from her "Charlie" perfume commercials. "She'll add class to the show, she'll be great," everyone declared, but a year later, Shelly was fired. The home audience didn't seem to be responding to her the way the producers thought they would.

Tanya Roberts replaced Shelly this season, playing Julie Richards. Although she's starred in several plays and guested on many shows, this is her first regular series. Tanya stands 5 feet, 7½ inches tall, has reddish-brown hair, and light blue

eyes. She was born in New York City and is married to television writer Barry Roberts.

Will the new angel make it? Will the other angels stay? So far, Cheryl Ladd seems content with the series, and although Jaclyn seemed a bit dissatisfied with the series last year, she's back again with nothing but good words to say for the show and her two co-stars.

And so, the "once-upon-a-time" story of *Charlie's Angels* goes on for another year.

SHAWN STEVENS:
EIGHT ISn't ENOUGH

His light brown hair falls softly around his face. His blue eyes look deeply into yours when he speaks to you. His voice is soft, yet self-assured, and he knows how to put you at ease.

His name is Shawn Stevens, the 22-year-old actor who has a recurring role on *Eight Is Enough*. He plays Jack, the college boyfriend of Connie Newton's character, Elizabeth. But though he loves the show and being a part of it is exciting for him, it isn't enough to keep Shawn Stevens content.

"I love working more than anything. If I'm idle more than a couple of days I start to get restless. I begin to feel like I'm wasting time, like I'm not expressing myself."

To keep from feeling that way, Shawn's been working on winning a record contract, and with a voice like his it shouldn't be hard. He studied voice and music while in high school and can really belt out a song.

Recently, he won the lead role in a movie, *Savage Harvest*, about wild animals that trap a family in their home in the jungle. "I auditioned for the part and then they called me back a couple of times to have me read the script again. I didn't know if I had the part or not until they called one afternoon a couple of weeks later and said it was all mine. I was at home when I got the phone call and I think I shouted with delight so loudly the entire neighborhood heard me."

Although Shawn doesn't have a steady girl-friend, he is seen about town quite a bit with one particular lady on his arm. She's his grandmother, whom he's very close to. "You could say she's one of my best friends," Shawn says fondly, "and she started me off on my career by taking me down to the community theater when I was just a little kid in Morristown, New Jersey."

Although he doesn't appear on *Eight Is Enough* every week, Shawn's been getting a lot of mail because of his role so you'll probably be seeing more and more of him as the fall season moves along. "I've known Adam Rich for a few years and I always have a lot of fun with him on the set. He's a real practical joker, and I'm not, but I'm learning to be!"

Shawn also has become good friends with Willie Aames who plays Tommy Bradford. "I think it's because we both have a big interest in music," Shawn states. "Willie's got a band called Paradise and I've heard them play at shows around town. Music is important to Willie just like it is to me."

OH! THOSE NIGHTTIME SOAPS

It was actually the situation comedy *Soap* that started the trend in nighttime soap operas, but since that hit series is just a take-off on how complicated daytime soap operas can be, it really doesn't count. A soap opera is a dramatic series full of twists and turns, and just like the daytime soap operas, it continues with the same story line each time it's aired.

Dallas is the series that started a trend in nighttime soap operas. It was followed by *Knots Landing* and this season's *Flamingo Road*.

Larry Hagman is the star of *Dallas*, although there are more than 10 other continuing roles. He plays the mean Mr. J.R. Ewing, though in real life he's nothing like J.R. Patrick Duffy, whom you might recall from *The Man from Atlantis*, is a little more like his character, Bobby—kind, considerate—the good guy. What makes *Dallas* different from the two other soaps is that the plots revolve around the family—and most of the characters are related.

On *Knots Landing* Ted Shackelford is Gary Ewing (yes—the name's the same; Ted played J.R. and Bobby's brother on *Dallas* until *Knots Landing* became a spinoff from the show). And Joan Van Ark plays his wife. Their best friends, Constance McCashin and John Pleshette, played by Michele Lee and Don Murray, live next door, and most of the shows revolve around these four.

Flamingo Road is new to the lineup this year. It got its start as a movie-of-the-week for television, and stars Tom Harmon (remember him from *240-Robert*?) as a young town sheriff about to go into politics. The town is practically owned and ruled by the wealthy Weldon family.

Will the popularity of prime-time soaps go on? So far it looks like they are on a hot streak, and with *Dallas* leading the way (don't forget—the first show of the 1980 season was one of the highest rated shows ever aired), they could be on a long time. The reason *Dallas* rated so high that first week in September was because the show ended the previous spring with J.R. being shot and rushed to the hospital. All summer fans wondered who had shot J.R. and why. It kept them all on edge until September, when everyone tuned in to find out! That's probably the way *Dallas, Knot's Landing,* and *Flamingo Road* will end this season too—keeping the viewers coming back for more!

MICHAEL YOUNG:
Host with the Most

Kids Are People, Too might be a show presented especially for kids, but according to the popular host of this Sunday morning talk show, a lot of the mail he receives starts out, "I'm not a kid, I'm an adult, but I enjoy your show too."

How does the 6'1" Michael feel about that? "I think it's wonderful, and it proves kids can teach grown-ups a thing or two, just as adults can teach young people."

Along with popular shows like Johnny Carson's *Tonight Show* and *The Muppets*, *Kids* is one of the few shows that attracts top name stars as guests. That's quite an accomplishment, and Michael's not shy about admitting how proud it makes him feel. "Not only do we have stars like Henry Winkler, Cindy Williams, Shaun Cassidy, Scott Baio, Robby Benson, Valerie Harper, Joyce DeWitt, Christopher Reeve, and Cheryl Tiegs, but sports figures like Reggie Jackson, famous lawyers, doctors, and even politicians."

But more than the guest stars each week, it's Michael himself who attracts the viewers. Sure he's good at making the guests feel relaxed and he asks interesting questions, but mostly it's his attitude toward his young audience. They feel that Michael cares about them; and they're right, he does.

"I guess I've always gotten along well with young people," Michael says. "I don't see them as just kids or someone too young to have any good ideas or be interesting to talk with. In fact, I find them very intelligent and aware of what's happening in the world. If you treat them with respect and concern, you'll get it back in return."

Michael's attitude toward young people has helped boost the ratings of *Kids*, and the show has won many awards, including an Emmy as the "Most Outstanding Children's Entertainment Series" of 1979. Chances are it will win again in 1980, especially with a host like Michael.

Born in Montgomery, Alabama, to Betty and Sam Young, Michael spent his growing-up years in the Orient, Europe, and Washington, D.C. His father is a career Air Force officer and had to travel to American bases all over the world.

Unlike lots of stars today, Michael didn't decide on a career in acting until he was already in his twenties. On the spur of the moment he auditioned for a play and won a small role. He supported himself working as a sales clerk and a waiter while he developed his acting skills.

Originally, *Kids* was filmed in New York, but last year the show moved to Hollywood to be closer to the big name talent they like to invite on the show. "Still," Michael says, "filming in New York turned out to be easier, so this year we moved back. Our program is so popular that most of the talent we'd like as guests will fly to New York to do the show."

The series is taped before a live audience, with the young people participating in the interviews by asking questions. Although the show is aired only one day a week, taping takes place Monday through Friday, and two shows are done each day. "That's because once you've got all the equipment set up to tape, it's easier to keep going.

It's hard work doing it all in one day, but this way we get longer vacations because we can complete twenty-six shows in about three weeks."

Although Michael loved working in California, he feels New York is just as exciting a place. "Maybe even more so," he says. "Besides, when filming is over I can always hop on a plane and stay in California for a couple of months. This way I get the best of both worlds."

STONEY JACKSON:
White Shadow's New Heartthrob!

"I've got such an outgoing personality, I never feel uncomfortable in a crowd," smiles handsome, 18-year-old Stoney Jackson, who plays Jessie on *The White Shadow*. And that's part of the reason he won the role of the 16-year-old, 10th-grade ladies' man.

"My character is very popular with the girls, and you might even call him a playboy," Stoney says. "And when I went to audition for the role, my aggressive attitude convinced them I was the right guy for the part!"

But, though Stoney's TV character loves chasing the girls, in real life Stoney admits he doesn't come on that strong. "Especially when I meet a girl for the first time, or I see a girl at a roller skating rink and I think she'd be nice to get to know. I usually go over, say hello, and ask her questions about school, what she likes to do. I'd never rush over and just ask someone out like Jessie would."

Roller skating rinks are one of the places in which dark-haired, brown-eyed Stoney hangs out. In fact, he starred in the skating movie, *Roller Boogie*, with Linda Blair, and is one of the best skaters around. "I love whizzing around on wheels," Stoney says. "In fact, I love whizzing around. I was never one to sit still for long, and through the years I've studied shotokan karate, judo, boxing, and a little gymnastics."

Actually, Stoney's a bit modest when it comes to talking about himself. He also swims and dives, throws the javelin, plays basketball, and loves to dance. "If I hear music, my feet are ready to dance," he laughs.

Since he's been working on *The White Shadow,* Stoney finds he doesn't have as much time for all of his outside interests. "Filming the show generally takes from seven in the morning until six at night—minimum! Then, by the time I get home, have something to eat, and relax a while, it's time to study my script for the next day. I try to get in bed by eleven P.M., the latest."

Although Stoney lives with his family in their five-bedroom home in Diamond Bar, California, he's been looking for an apartment of his own, closer to the studio. "It's over an hour's drive to work, and that means I've got to get up earlier and fight all the traffic," he sighs. "I love my family, we're very close, but they agree it would be a lot easier for me to live in town during the months I'm filming."

Born in Richmond, Virginia, on February 27, 1962, Stoney also lived in Maryland and Florida while growing up, and he played the drums in the high school band. "I've always loved music and I also play a little guitar and sing." Again, Stoney's being a bit modest. He not only sings, but sings well and writes songs too. Several record companies are showing interest in recording him, so it might not be long before you'll be hearing him singing on the radio.

As friendly and outspoken as he is, Stoney has a quiet side as well. "I love going for walks along the beach or in the park. When my family moved to California in 1976, I spent hours at the beach just watching the ocean or strolling along the shore. It's a good place to go when you want to reflect on your life or just be alone with your thoughts."

But then a twinkle appears in Stoney's eyes and he laughs a little. "It's a good place to go with a girl, too. The beach is romantic, and what's more romantic than walking in the moonlight with the stars above you and the waves pounding softly in the background?"

Stoney is one of the new guys on *The White Shadow* this season. Only Tim Van Patten, Byron Stewart, Kevin Hooks, and, of course, the star Ken Howard remain from last year's lineup. "They decided they wanted some new faces on the show and I'm glad they did," Stoney says. "Otherwise I might not be here. It's a great show to work on and we all get along fine."

Although Stoney hasn't been on *The White Shadow* very long yet, his fan mail is already starting to come in. Before this series he was a semi-regular on *Eight Is Enough* and has done guest appearances on *What's Happening* and *Quincy*.

"Fan mail is exciting," he declares. "It's a wonderful feeling to know so many people care about you." Well, it's easy to care about a guy as magical as Stoney. Don't you agree?

TV QUESTIONS
AND ANSWERS

What's the truth? What's happening? Here are the answers to the questions you've been asking the most.

Q: *Maude* was one of my favorite TV shows, especially since beautiful Adrienne Barbeau was in it. Is she married?

A: Yes. Adrienne is married to the successful film director of scary movies, John Carpenter. Two of his box office hits were *Halloween* and *The Fog*. In the latter, Adrienne had the leading role.

Q: I really enjoyed the three-part mini-series *Moviola*. Who was the actress who played the role of Carole Lombard?

A: Sharon Gless played Lombard. She's done numerous TV shows—among the most recent are *Centennial* and *The Last Convertible*.

Q: Is it true the actress who plays Lorie Brooks on *The Young and the Restless* used to date Henry Winkler?

A: Yes. Jamie Lyn Bauer and "The Fonz" dated steadily for about six months in 1978.

Q: Why don't they cancel *Charlie's Angels* instead of trying out all these actresses?

A: *Charlie's Angels* is still one of the top ten shows on television. The ratings continue to be favorable regardless of all the actresses coming and going. People still tune in to watch the three pretty angels!

Q: How old is Loni Anderson's daughter?

A: Daughter Dede, whom Loni raised while

putting herself through college after her divorce, has turned sweet 16!

Q: What else has Stefanie Powers starred in besides *Hart to Hart*?

A: Stefanie's first series, in 1966, was *The Girl from U.N.C.L.E.*, which was about two secret agents working for the United States Government. Her co-star was Noel Harrison, son of actor Rex Harrison. She was in another series, *The Feather and Father Gang*, a few years ago and was featured in the mini-series *Washington: Behind Closed Doors*.

Q: Is Scott Baio an only child? How old is he, and does he still live at home?

A: Scott has a brother Steven and a sister Stephanie who are 22-year-old twins. Scott is 19 and all the Baios live together in their two-story home in the Hollywood Hills.

Q: Does Joyce DeWitt have any ambition to do TV movies and films, or is she content with *Three's Company*?

A: Like most actresses, Joyce has a strong desire to branch out and do other things with her career. Although she's extremely happy with her hit show, she has been looking around for other projects, especially a Broadway show. Along with her boyfriend/manager Stuart Ehrlich, her efforts have been in vain so far, but they're not giving up and know the right script will come along soon.

Q: What are the names of all the movies John

Travolta has starred in? Why did he leave *Welcome Back, Kotter*, and will he ever do a TV series again?

A: "Never" is a long time, and though John says he prefers to not do television, lots of actors have changed their minds over the years. John left *Kotter* to do films, and except for *Moment by Moment* with Lily Tomlin, they've all been big hits. The others were *Carrie*, *Grease*, *Saturday Night Fever*, and his latest, *Urban Cowboy*.

Q: Does Pam Dawber have a steady boyfriend? I never hear anything about her private life.

A: Pam likes to keep her private life private, but she has been steady with handsome Phil Coccioletti for almost two years. He's an actor/model whose face is recognizable from his many Benson & Hedges cigarette billboard ads across the country. Pam and Phil met in New York when they filmed an ad together for a convertible sofa bed. It wasn't until years later, when they met again in Hollywood, that they started dating.

Q: Did Isabel Sanford do any acting before she shot to fame on *The Jeffersons*?

A: Isabel came from a non-acting family and spent years trying to make it in the business. The only one of seven children to survive infancy, Isabel was raised by a foster family in Harlem after both her parents died. As a little girl she dreamt about people applauding her and realized at a very young age that she wanted to be an actress. During high school she was in several plays and even appeared as a man in a Chinese opera! In the evenings she performed in small clubs around Harlem, doing monologues and singing. In the early 1960s Isabel packed her bags and three children from an unsuccessful marriage, and headed for Los Angeles. She managed to get a few small acting roles but worked as a key-punch operator when her luck was down. It wasn't until she landed the 1965 play *The Amen Corner*, which took her to Broadway and critical acclaim, that she started getting offers. From there she went on to play the maid in *Guess Who's Coming to Dinner* and was a semi-regular on *The Carol Burnett Show*. Norman Lear called in 1971 and she's been with *The Jeffersons* ever since!

Q: I can't remember the nickname Mr. De-Fazzio calls Laverne on *Laverne and Shirley*. Can you help?

A: Certainly—it's "Muffin."

Q: There is never any mention about Kristy and Jimmy McNichol's father. What happened to him?

A: Their father was a carpenter who walked out of the marriage when they were very young. Since then, mom Carollyn has been the backbone of the family, guiding the careers of Kristy and Jimmy. A third McNichol, Tommy, who is 15, lives with his maternal grandmother in Burbank and has no interest

in show business. Jimmy and his dad have recently had a reconciliation and are sharing a home in the San Fernando Valley.

Q: Do actors and actresses appearing on talk shows rehearse their lines ahead of time?

A: No, but they're usually briefed before the show on the various topics the host will ask them about. There is usually a practice run-through so everyone will know when to come onstage, where to sit, etc.

Q: Do the stars who appear on *American Bandstand* sing live?

A: No, all the performers on Dick Clark's afternoon weekend show lip-sync their hits. That means the record plays in the background, and they move their mouths to the words.

Q: What's Peter Barton doing now that he's not on *Shirley* anymore?

A: Peter isn't quite sure what direction he wants to take with his life. After the series was canceled, he moved back to New York for awhile. He did have a role in a proposed new series, *Three Eyes*, about three guys doing detective work, like Charlie's Angels do. The pilot didn't sell, however, and Peter went back to New York, where he's deciding whether to go back to modeling or to continue his education as a pharmaceutical major. He's still under contract to NBC-TV for several months, so if something comes up, he'll probably give Hollywood another shot.

Q: Is it true Grant Goodeve wants out of *Eight Is Enough*?

A: Not really out; he just wants his role to change a bit. He felt that having his character get married was a mistake, and he didn't feel involved enough each week. This season, his character, David Bradford, will get divorced, and Grant says he's looking forward to more chances to display his acting ability.

Q: I miss seeing Donny and Marie on TV. Is there any chance their show will be back?

A: No, no chance. *Donny and Marie* is seen in syndication in some cities, so check your local TV listings to see if your city is one. Donny and Marie have decided to pursue individual careers. Donny will be featured in two TV movies this season, and Marie is in Hollywood now, working on a series that might be aired in January. There will be a Donny and Marie (and family!) Christmas special, however.

Q: How long does a network give a new series to tell if it's a hit or not?

A: Most people believe new series aren't given a long enough try-out period. Some are pulled off the air after only two to five showings. Some series which are hits today (*All in the Family*, *WKRP in Cincinnati*, and *Benson* among them) started out with low ratings and were almost canceled. Luckily, someone gave them a chance.

Q: Is Parker Stevenson doing anything these days?

A: Since the cancellation of *The Hardy Boys* a couple of years ago, Parker hasn't been involved much in the entertainment area and hasn't kept in touch with anyone from the *Hardy Boys* days. He's seen every so often at Hollywood functions, so it looks as if show business is still in his blood. Maybe he'll be back this year.

Q: How tall is Wayne Rogers of *House Calls*?

A: He's 6′3″ tall. His co-star on the show, Lynn Redgrave, is 5′10″ and says it's wonderful working with an actor who is still an inch taller when she wears 3″ high heels.

Q: I've been watching *Shazam* on Saturday afternoons, and all the shows seem to be repeats from when the series was on several years ago. What's the story?

A: The shows are all repeats, but since it seems to be doing well in the ratings, there is a slight possibility they may call the cast back and film some new shows. Actor Michael Gray, who starred in the series, says he'd be willing to revive it.

Q: Is that Lynda Carter I see in advertisements for makeup?

A: Yes, it is. Lynda is the national spokesperson for Maybelline Cosmetics, just as Joyce DeWitt is for L'Eggs hosiery and Cheryl Ladd is for Wella Balsam. More and more actors and actresses of every age (George Burns plugs Visa/BankAmericard) are doing TV commercials (and often magazine and radio ads) in which they're themselves—not just acting a part. The big companies feel their sales will go up—and they have. Don't forget Donny and Marie for Hawaiian Punch, Sandy Duncan for Wheat Thins, and now Andy Gibb has agreed to represent Hawaiian Tropics suntan products.

Q: Why did they change the cast of *The White Shadow*?

A: Nobody knows the real answer to that. Acccording to Ira Angustain (he played Gomez), his agent asked for too much money so they dropped his contract. The network says they wanted to bring in some younger stars, but insiders on the set say there was a lot of friction between cast members.

34

GETTING TO KNOW DEAN BUTLER

Last season on *Little House on the Prairie*, you followed the meeting, romance, and courtship of Laura Ingalls, played by Melissa Gilbert, and Almonzo Wilder, played by Dean Butler. This season the romance continues, and eventually the two will marry on the popular series. The young man selected to capture Laura's heart on the TV screen is a 6'1", green-eyed blond, who is actually the opposite of what the real Almonzo looked liked. (Don't forget—the *Little House* characters are based on real people.) He couldn't be happier with his role, and his excitement seems to bubble over when he answers questions about the show and himself!

Q: HOW DID YOU GET THE ROLE OF AL-MONZO?

DEAN: Well, actually I was up for the role of Adam Kendall, the young man who married Mary Ingalls (Melissa Sue Anderson), but they thought I was too tall for her. When they were casting for Almonzo, they remembered me and called me in for an audition. I guess I was right for the part because I have that country-boy look.

Q: BUT THEY DIDN'T THINK YOU WERE TOO TALL FOR MELISSA GILBERT?

DEAN: Well, yes they did, but I guess everything else was right and they decided they could deal with that. Besides, Almonzo was actually ten years older than Laura, so my being taller just emphasizes the age difference, since I'm not really ten years older than Melissa.

Q: WHAT WAS YOUR FIRST DAY ON THE SET LIKE?

DEAN: Scary. On the first show my character arrives in town with his sister, Eliza Jane, who is the school teacher, and we were both a little bit tense. I wanted to impress everyone and do well. In the scene we're riding in a wagon, but suddenly the wind blew my hat off (that wasn't in the script!), and I quickly grabbed for it and forgot my lines. To make matters worse, the horses pulling the wagon got startled and took off down the road with us in it!

Q: HOW DID MICHAEL LANDON AND EVERYONE ELSE ON THE SET REACT TO THAT?

DEAN: They were wonderful, and I felt a lot better. Everyone laughed and cheered and put me right at ease. Working on the show has been a very pleasant, warm experience.

Q: HOW DO YOU GET ALONG WITH MELISSA GILBERT?

DEAN: I have a wonderful working relationship with her. When I first did my scenes with her I was a little bit in awe of her. I mean, here I was acting with one of America's favorite little girls. People have watched her grow up on television, and I knew they'd be watching me—making sure I wasn't going to be bad for her.

Q: BUT IT'S JUST A TELEVISION SERIES.

DEAN: True, but people tend to relate to someone in a role like Laura. Everyone loves her, adores her, and wants her to be happy even if it's just a script!

Q: WHAT DO YOU THINK OF MELISSA PROFESSIONALLY?

DEAN: She's the top. She has a special quality that's so natural, and she's really involved in each scene. She's got such a great memory too. If we have to reshoot a scene, she'll tell me where I had my hand, or if my left foot was in front of my right the first time around. Directors love that in an actor or actress. Michael Landon is good that way too, and I hope I'll be.

Q: WHAT WOULD YOU SAY ARE YOUR BEST AND WORST CHARACTERISTICS?

DEAN: I think my best quality is my self-motivation and drive. I'm a doer and I'm always trying to improve myself, learn something new. On the bad side, I tend to procrastinate a lot. I put things off until tomorrow.

Q: WHAT WOULD YOU DO IF YOU COULDN'T BE AN ACTOR?

DEAN: Probably be a radio disc jockey. Or a director. I'd like to write or direct something like *Little House on the Prairie*. I would try to surround myself with quality people who would be a real team, just like on the series.

Q: DO YOU GET ANY FAN MAIL?

DEAN: Yes, and I love it. I write back to fans a lot. If I get a letter that seems like someone is really interested in getting to know me, I sit down and whip out a quick response. It's nice the way fans take time to write you, to let you know what they feel about you or your performance.

Q: HOW DO YOU FEEL ABOUT BEING ON THE SERIES?

DEAN: Terrific, but mostly because I've discovered viewers like me as Almonzo. Sure I'm acting for myself, because it's what I've chosen as a career, but I'm doing it for the audience also, because I want someone to enjoy what I'm doing. That's why I wanted to do *Little House* in the first place. It's the kind of show where the viewer can sit down, have a good cry, and even learn a lesson along the way.

PHILIP McKEON:
Alice's Angel

"The only thing missing on the set of *Alice* is a dog," laughs Philip McKeon, who plays Tommy Hyatt on the top-rated series. "I'm such an animal lover, I always enjoy having a dog or cat around."

But even though *Alice* is a "no pets allowed" set, Philip more than makes up for it when he goes home each night. "I've got a female German shepherd named George. She's gorgeous, about two-and-a-half years old with little ears that flap all over the place when she runs. She loves the beach, and when I take her there she chases after the seagulls."

According to Philip, everyone in the McKeon household is an animal lover, and that includes his sister Nancy, who is 14. "Even George likes animals," Philip shrugs. "Especially cats. We've got a cat called Kaz—a little black thing who loves sleeping on the end of the bed. If I turn over during the night, he tries to bite my toes. I can feel him stalking my feet across the bed, and then bam, he pounces!"

"Actually," explains Philip, "George's full name is Georgette, but she doesn't seem to like it as much as George. She was named when I got her from an organization called Actors and Others for Animals. Every year they have a big celebrity auction and fair to raise money to help homeless pets. They have a staff and they spay or neuter the animals and try to find good homes for them. I was at the auction a couple of years ago and thought the organization was a good one,

41

so when I decided to get a dog, that's where I went.''

Philip also believes a dog or cat should be part of the family. "Ever since the first night I got George she's slept in my room. She sleeps by the side of the bed and Kaz sleeps on it. The two get along great. You should see them play. Kaz will lie down and George comes over and nips his tail. The cat hides under the covers and the dog can't find him. It's a sight to see—that little cat frustrating this big dog.''

Philip laughs and his blue eyes twinkle when he talks about his pets. "Poor Kaz was a stray. Practically starving. We live around the corner from a market and Kaz was hanging out, a tiny kitten only a few weeks old. He was trying to find food in the trash cans. I stuffed him inside my jacket and fed him some turkey since it was a couple of days after Thanksgiving and we had a lot of left-overs. When I let him loose back at the store, he wouldn't stay. He kept following me back home and climbed up the screen at the back door. He dug his claws in and wouldn't let go, so I finally told my folks the cat must be ours. From the start George and Kaz got along fine. In fact, they like each other so much they don't like to be separated, and when the family goes on trips we have to board the two pets together.''

It might be hard to find a family closer and happier than the McKeons. Philip was born on November 11, 1964, in New York, and even as a toddler he was happy most of the time. In fact, his pediatrician called him "Smiling Jack." At an early age he began his career appearing in television commercials, which led to a role in the Barbra Streisand movie, *Up the Sandbox*.

Films led to Broadway, where Philip performed in the dramatic play, *Jason and Medea*, and then finally came the role on *Alice*, which Philip almost didn't take! "I knew accepting the part would change my life forever. We would have to move from New York to California, and I'd have to say good-bye to familiar places, friends, and a lot of relatives."

Luckily for Philip's fans, his desire for a career in acting was strong. And though he's been living in Southern California now for four years, he hasn't lost touch with anyone he knew in New York, and the family goes home for a visit a couple of times each year.

"Besides," Philip adds with a big grin, "I made so many new friends here there's no time to dwell on the past. The *Alice* cast is terrific. We share our joys, and we're almost like a real family ourselves. I think that comes across on the television screen. I think our relationship with each other is what made the show click with viewers."

THOSE OLDIES BUT GOODIES
. . . and where they are today!

Maybe you watch reruns of shows that were popular a few years ago, shows like *I Love Lucy*, *The Partridge Family*, *The Brady Bunch*. Some of them were popular 10 years ago, or more — *I Love Lucy* was the biggest hit of all in the 1950s. What happened to the people who starred in these shows? Are they still in Hollywood? Here's the scoop on some of your favorites!

THE PARTRIDGE FAMILY:
David Cassidy's Still In Town

Every week millions of viewers tuned in to *The Partridge Family* to follow the fun, but mostly to see David Cassidy in action. *The Partridge Family* was top TV fare in the 1970–73 TV seasons, and mostly because 19-year-old David was the reigning teen idol. The Partridge Family released albums and single records and so did David, as a solo act. Ten years have passed since the Partridges were America's number one family, but the series has been rerun all over the United States for a long time.

In 1974 the show went off the air, and David spent the next year or two touring all over the world doing concerts. Then suddenly, he retired from show business, moved to a beach community in California, and went into seclusion. "I was tired. I was disappointed. I thought people had used me to make money and really didn't care about me as David, the guy. I needed time to be alone and think about where my life was going," David recalls.

Eight months later David met Kay Lenz, and she offered her strength and support. "I learned to care about people again, to trust them, and I owe a lot to her." David and Kay were married, and today they live in the hills of Hollywood.

David starred in a short-lived series, *Undercover Man*, and made appearances on shows like *Fantasy Island* and this fall's TV movie, *The Night the City Screamed*.

"But what I'm mostly happy about," says David, "is my recording career. I've been in the studio for the last couple of months and I should have an album out shortly. Singing was always something I loved, and it's a wonderful feeling to be involved with it again.''

And the rest of the Partridges? Well, you know Shirley Jones has kept busy with her career in TV movies and films, and last year she had another series, *Shirley*, with Peter Barton. Son Shaun (you already know a lot about him!) is married now; 18-year-old Patrick Cassidy is getting ready to enter the show business world and is looking for a good TV or movie script. The youngest son, Ryan, is now 15 and still going to school.

Susan Dey has been married to her agent, Lenny Hirshan, for several years, and they have a two-year-old daughter, Sarah. Susan still appears in lots of television movies. Right now she's content being a part-time actress. ''My family comes first,'' she says definitely.

Suzanne Crough, who played Tracy, just graduated from high school and plans to go full speed ahead with her acting career. In between, she's made many guest appearances.

Danny Bonaduce stars in *Vera*, a feature film with Martin Sheen. He's been doing guest appearances through the years on many series, including *Eight Is Enough* and *Fantasy Island*. Twenty-year-old Danny still has flaming red hair and those famous freckles, as well as a devilish grin. ''I still get cast as Danny Partridge types,'' sighs Danny. ''He was so precocious. But I guess there's a little of him in me still,'' he admits.

Brian Forster, who played Chris (he replaced

Jeremy Gelbwaks, who was Chris the first year), is the only ex-Partridge who decided against a career in show business. He's 20 now and enrolled as a veterinary major in college. He always did love animals. He likes music too (remember he played drums on the show), and says his second choice for a career would be as a sound engineer.

THAT'S THE WAY THEY ALL BECAME THE BRADY BUNCH . . .

Those are the familliar words to the Bradys' theme song, and this show was just as popular as *The Partridge Family*, in the early 1970s.

"I really had a wonderful time doing that show and playing Marcia," recalls Maureen McCormick, whose latest film is *The Boys*. "Since then, I've starred in a lot of TV movies, and films, including *Skatetown, U.S.A.*, and I've been taking voice lessons and singing back-up for rock musician Eddy Money. I hope to have a record of my own released this year." Knowing Maureen, she will.

Barry Williams (who played Greg), now 25, admits he was sorry to see the show canceled after several successful years. "Since that time I've continued my schooling and pursued an acting and singing career. I've been touring the country doing all kinds of plays, and I've made a record. As soon as a record company wants to sign a contract—I'm ready."

Maybe you already know what Chris Knight,

who starred as Peter Brady, is up to. Last summer he starred in *Joe's World*, but when *The Brady Bunch* went off the air, he decided to quit show business for a while. "I went to high school, and then on to college for a couple of years," says the 22-year-old, who's since let his hair go curly and developed his muscles with weight lifting. "One day while on campus, it all suddenly came back to me: how much fun it was, how much personal satisfaction being an actor gave me. I decided to get back in the business, and I did that, too!"

Pretty Eve Plumb, who starred as Jan, is the only ex-Brady who got married—so far. The blond 20-year-old was wed over a year ago to cameraman Rick Mansfield. Eve's been acting steadily since the Bradys were canceled, and co-starred in *Little Women* with Susan Dey. She even has her own production company now, called Fleur de Lis Productions.

Susan Olson was little Cindy Brady, and the 18-year-old just graduated from high school last June. She hopes to really get involved with acting now that her high school education is behind her. Susan would like to enroll in college too, and study drama.

Like Brian Forster from *The Partridge Family*, Mike Lookinland chose not to pursue a show business career. "When my days of playing Bobby Brady were over, I just settled back into being a regular kid." He's just turned 19 years old and enrolled in college, though he's not sure what career goals he'll set for himself yet!

SHORTS SHORTS SHORTS SHORTS SHORTS SHORTS SHORTS

Things you didn't know about your favorites

GREGORY HARRISON
Dr. Gonzo Gates in
Trapper John, M.D.

He's just under 6' tall, weighs 170 pounds, has expressive hazel eyes and curly dark brown hair. Besides that, he's very talented as an actor, writes songs and poetry, sings and plays the guitar. But what's more important, he truly cares about people and spends a lot of his free time helping struggling young actors and actresses get started.

That's because Greg remembers how hard it was for him to break into show business. "I was born and raised on Catalina Island off the coast of California, and although I did some theater during high school and later when I got out of the Army, I never had any formal training. I came to Hollywood and didn't know a soul. I practically starved for six years, living off of seventeen-cent boxes of macaroni and cheese. I enrolled in an acting workshop. But a lot of getting parts in the beginning depends upon getting your name known, and you need friends who can help you. That's why today when I meet people trying to break into the business I try to help. I offer advice, read scenes with them, and direct them in audition scenes at my house. If I believe in them and they've got the talent, I'll put in a word for them with a producer or casting agent. It's important that people help each other."

With that kind of attitude, no wonder Greg is so convincing in his role as Dr. Gates. They've both got the biggest smiles on their faces when helping others!

WILLIE AAMES
(Tommy Bradford on Eight Is Enough)

How did Albert Willie Upton end up Willie Aames? "Well, we got stuck in a jam when I first started in the industry," Willie explains. "There was already an actor registered with the Screen Actor's Guild named Willie Upton, and you can't have two people with the same name. My agent at the time suggested Aames—with two A's, so we could always be at the beginning of a list!"

A lot has happened to Willie since that day. His earliest parts were in TV commercials, followed by guest shots on shows like *The Odd Couple*, *Medical Center*, and *The Courtship of Eddie's Father*. He starred on the series *Swiss Family Robinson* in 1975, in several Walt Disney movies, and finally hit it big with *Eight Is Enough*.

"Now that my acting career is going along so well, I've gotten back to my first love: music. I'm spending more and more time with it. I've got a band, Paradise, and we're working on putting together an album." In fact, Willie loves music so much, he says if it ever came down to choosing between acting and singing, he'd take singing. And that's not all that's happened to Willie. Several months ago he married Vicki Averbach, and since he loves children so much, don't be surprised if they start a family soon.

Willie's also been keeping busy as a spokesperson for the Right Track Organization, a group whose members include celebrities like John Travolta, Diana Canova, and Eddie Mekka. The purpose of the group is to fight teenage drug addiction. "In fact," Willie says, "the goal is to get kids to self-determinedly decide NOT to be on drugs."

It takes someone who really cares about people, especially young people, to devote time to a cause like this, and Willie is definitely that kind of guy. Just ask his friends, family, and co-stars on *Eight Is Enough*. "There's never enough you can do for others." Willie proclaims.

TOM WOPAT
(Luke Duke On
The Dukes of Hazzard)

"I used to have to get up at the break of dawn to milk the cows before I went to school," reflects Tom Wopat as he casually leans back in his chair, crossing his long legs in front of him. "I was raised on a dairy farm in Lodi, Wisconsin, and that's a long way from Hollywood. At the time I never dreamed I'd one day be starring on a hit television series that takes place in a town like Lodi—peaceful, lazy, real down-home."

During his high school years, Tom was more interested in playing football and being on the track team than in acting, though he did find time to play in the band and sing in the chorus. It wasn't until he enrolled at the University of Wisconsin that he got interested in theater, but since he was a music major, he spent more time playing guitar and singing. "After a while I left the university to pursue a music career. I formed a rock group with some friends, and for a couple of years we traveled around the country performing wherever we could. I was lead singer and guitarist."

Then one day, when the group finished performing in Michigan, Tom decided to stay on and join a theater group. "I appeared in plays like *Pajama Game* and *Annie Get Your Gun*, and realized I truly enjoyed acting. Next thing I did was move to New York and get an agent." That was only the beginning for the 6' tall actor with big, blue eyes who has now hit it big in Hollywood. "I've got an apartment in New York, one in Los Angeles, and my family home in Lodi," he smiles contentedly. "I even splurged and bought not one motorcycle, but three—so I could have one no matter where I was living—even back home on the farm."

JOHN SCHNEIDER
(Bo Duke on
The Dukes of Hazzard)

Strong, tall, good-looking, blond-haired, and blue-eyed—you already know that describes John

Schneider, and he agrees. "But being handsome can have its drawbacks," he smiles, and his blue eyes twinkle under his soft, fluffy hair. "You can get stereotyped and never play anything but good, wholesome, down-to-earth guys. Not that there's anything wrong with that, but an actor likes to portray lots of different characters."

John is one star who really cares about his fans. "I get along very well with people and I never forget, even if I sometimes have to remind myself, that I'm in this for people. If it weren't for my fans watching the show, where would I be? The feeling I get when I know someone is enjoying my work on *Dukes* is the most wonderful thing I know.''

It's true too. All John's friends and family will be the first to say it. "John is like someone you'd *want* to have as a friend," say his TV producers. "That's how his character comes off and that's why just about everyone loves Bo Duke.''

John says he especially loves meeting people on the street. "It's a nice feeling when someone runs up to you and acts like they've known you all their life. It makes me feel very comfortable that they don't treat me like an actor or a star— just an ordinary person.''

John spent a lot of the summer when the show was on hiatus traveling around the country on promotional tours. "It's great to get out there and meet fans. I don't mind signing autographs either.''

You know that's true, because John's been known to stick around signing autographs when other stars have left. In fact, at an autograph party on behalf of a children's hospital and cerebral palsy fund, John performed on stage (yes, he's a great singer!) before 12,000 people until one A.M. Then, he stuck around and signed autographs until four A.M.

There aren't many stars who will do that, and maybe it's one reason John has such a faithful following. "My religion," he says, "is trying to make people happy." And he does.

SCOTT BAIO
(ChaChi on Happy Days)

The cream-colored Mercedes drives slowly
past the guard booth, and Scott Baio leans out
the window a little to say good morning to the
security guard on duty. He turns left, then makes
another left, and pulls up in front of his trailer
dressing room right outside the sound stage where
Happy Days is filmed on the Paramount Studios'
lot.

It's the first day back at work after almost six
months off. Of course, Scott wasn't exactly on

vacation during those months. He did guest roles on shows like *Boomer* and *Goodtime Girls*, and even flew back to New York to appear on *Kids Are People, Too*. And he did a lot of co-hosting on talk shows like *Merv Griffin*—and guesting on other talk shows.

He also enrolled in an cinematography class at college, and almost every weekend did personal appearances at amusement parks and fairs all over the country as part of a teen variety act.

"I had a really incredible summer, though," reflects the good-looking, young actor as he gets out of his car and opens the door of his dressing room. (Inside it's decorated with lots of gifts fans have given him over the years: a couch, a television, a desk for writing, and a closet with a full-length mirror. "I spent a lot of time swimming and working on my tan, and I loved the class I took. I'm really interested in how cameras work and I learned a great deal."

Scott also helped his dad Mario build a shelter for their homing pigeons. "We've got over fifty of them now," Scott says, picking up the script lying on the desk and flipping it to the page where ChaChi walks over to Fonzie. "Hey, Fonz, I've got a problem," he starts reading, then laughs. "Those pigeons caused me a bit of trouble this summer. We had one guy who was a bit crazy— his instincts were off. He was always flying into things, or getting caught in the underbrush in the hills by our home. One day he got caught in some bushes and was cooing like crazy, so I climbed up the hill to rescue him. I had been sunning at the pool, so I was just wearing a swim suit. Well, as it turned out there was poison oak in the hills, and lucky me got it all over! The pigeon was safe and sound, but I sure wasn't.''

Scott's family will attest to that. It took three weeks for the condition to clear up, and Scott had to cancel all the interviews and photo sessions he had set up during that time.

"It's awful," he smiles looking back on it now. "Scratch, scratch, scratch, but you're not supposed to. It's misery time. The pigeon got a better deal, because we set it free in an area where it wouldn't bump into so many things."

Scott says the first day back on the set after hiatus is always a lot of fun. "It's more like a reunion," he states. "First everyone talks about what they did, there's a lot of hugging and kissing, and after we read through the script one time we all take off for a big welcome back lunch. It really is a happy day," he adds, getting up from the couch where he'd been sitting. "Sorry I've got to go, but the director is waiting," he calls back as he heads towards the set. "See you around!" We'll see you around too, Scott. Every Tuesday on those wonderful *Happy Days*.

FELICE SCHACHTER
AND LISA WHELCHEL
The Facts of Their Lives

Take one 5′6″, 100-pound, dark-haired, green-eyed, 17-year-old. Add talent, charm, personal-

photo/(Michael Childers)

ity, and intelligence, and what do you have? An actress-model whom a leading photographer termed the most beautiful girl in the world: Felice Schachter.

But though people say she's a very special young lady (and she is!), Felice shrugs and seriously insists she's just a normal teenager. "That's why I enjoy my role on *Facts of Life* so much. My character, Nancy, is basically a lot like I am, and she's boy-crazy too. Just like me!"

But there are other things that make Felice a lot like Nancy. They're both sweet, down-to-earth, wholesome girls whom friends describe as genuine, nice, and unaware of just how pretty they really are.

Both of them enjoy school too. In fact, Felice is a straight-A student and recently enrolled at Harvard University to study psychology. "I'm very good at psychoanalyzing people," she declares. "I don't think I would ever let fame get to me because I try to be aware of where people and myself are coming from. I like to break down people's actions, their feelings, and again, mine included, and discover the reason they're doing or saying what they are.

"Originally I wanted to be a dancer, and I was dedicated to doing it six days a week, four hours a day. But dancers don't get that much recognition, and I thought that acting would bring me more notice," says the outspoken Felice. "But I'm really interested in developing my talent. That's more important than becoming famous."

Felice has been in show business almost since birth! She was featured in a TV commercial for babies, and by the age of one had appeared in many of them, including Pampers and Ivory Snow. By the age of six she was one of the country's leading models.

But then there were some hard times ahead for Felice. "I was in a near-fatal automobile crash, which broke most of the major bones in my body and caused severe internal injuries. I was in a toe-to-neck cast for four months and underwent numerous operations and rehabilitative therapy."

Her determination and constant encouragement from her family helped Felice make a miraculous recovery, and 13 months after the accident she was studying ballet, piano, and tap. During the next several years she danced with the New York City Ballet Company, and in 1975 won lead roles in two off-Broadway productions. The next year she was featured in the mini-series,

The Adams Chronicles, guest-starred on many series, and two years ago began her role as Nancy on *Facts of Life*, a spin-off from *Diff'rent Strokes*.

Despite her busy schedule, Felice is basically a "homebody," she says. She shares a large house in Jamaica Estates, New York, with her mother and two sisters, Simone, age 16, and 14-year-old Janine. Both sisters are also top models and actresses.

Somehow Felice also manages to pursue many other interests. "I love to read, and one of my favorite things to do on a rainy day is curl up with a good book and a cup of hot chocolate and spend the day reading. I also love crossword puzzles, playing pinball, and going out," she admits with a sparkle in her eye. "I wish I had a little more time to date, but I guess you could say I'm very career-oriented. There will always be time for boys after I get myself established."

Music is another of Felice's interests, and right now she likes New Wave music. She's also into Rod Stewart and the Rolling Stones. "I love going to rock concerts," she proclaims, "and I get so excited when I have a chance to meet a performer."

Still, she calls stars like Brooke Shields and Scott Baio her good friends, and you can add Leif Garrett, Matt Dillon, and Kristy McNichol to her list of acquaintances.

While filming *Facts of Life*, Felice lives on the West Coast with her grandparents, and though she enjoys the California life-style, she admits she always gets homesick for New York. "When

I'm doing the show all day long I don't have time to miss my family or friends, but when I get home at night I usually run up a big telephone bill talking to my mom and sisters."

But working with so many other girls on the show has given Felice a chance to make some good friends here, and she often goes to some of the Hollywood premieres and parties with Lisa Whelchel, who plays Blair on the series. The two especially share a common interest in roller skating, boys, and pizza.

Although Lisa didn't get started in her career quite so young as did Felice, she says she's wanted to be an actress since she was about eight years old. "My big break came when I tried out for the talent show at school and didn't make it! That got me thinking about what I could do to make it the next year, and I decided to try ventriloquism. I ordered a figure (you never call them dummies) from a catalog, complete with record and instruction booklet, and I got pretty good at it. The next year I won the talent show."

That started Lisa seriously on the road to an acting career. "I loved being on stage and performing, and when I read that Walt Disney Studios were holding auditions for young people to revive the *Mickey Mouse Club*, I applied."

Lisa passed her audition with flying colors and became one of the first members of *The New Mickey Mouse Club*, which aired in 1977. From there she starred in a Disney movie, *The Healer*, and then came the role as Blair on *Facts of Life*.

The 5'2", brown-eyed Lisa was born in Tuttlefield, Texas, on May 29, 1963, and though like Felice she lives in Southern California during filming season, she still calls Texas her home, and that's where she heads during hiatus.

As the saucy, independent, and often snobbish Blair, Lisa says she hopes the viewers at home don't think she's anything like her character. "Actually, Blair's not that bad. She just hasn't learned the importance of being nice and caring toward people. She puts on an act so everyone will think she's not afraid of anything. But she is, and that side comes out a lot too."

Certainly Lisa doesn't have to worry about anyone thinking she's just like Blair. She's one of the most popular young actresses in Hollywood, and everyone enjoys her company—and that's a fact!

ROBIN WILLIAMS
(Mork on Mork and Mindy)

"I get very upset when people say I've lost interest in *Mork and Mindy*," declares Robin Williams. "It's my first love." In fact, all summer long when Robin was in Malta (an island off the coast of Spain) filming his movie, *Popeye*, he called the network faithfully each week to check up on the show's summer ratings.

"It was quite an experience," says Robin. "As Popeye, I not only get to dance and sing, but even fight an octopus underwater. The special effects are incredible!"

photo/(Donald Sanders)

Of course, anything this talented actor/comedian does is bound to be incredible, and that's because Robin always gives his *all* for any project he's working on. Before heading to Malta to begin work on *Popeye*, he studied acrobatics (Popeye's pretty good with handstands and cartwheels), and dieted to lose 15 pounds. Since the movie is a musical, Robin also enrolled in voice classes and practiced dance as well.

This year, in between doing *Mork and Mindy*, Robin's developed a real interest in writing. "It's very hard to be funny in print," he sighs. "I can do it when I'm onstage or when I improvise on the set because I don't really think about it—it just comes straight out, kaboom! When I sit down at the typewriter I get scared. But you've got to confront those fears, solve them, and move on. When you do, it's an incredible feeling.

"Inspiration is like drilling for oil," Robin continues. "Sometimes I can think for hours and come up with nothing, and then in a few minutes it comes in waves. Maybe you have to go through those hours of time when nothing comes to you—the oil drill has to go so far to hit the oil—to get the times when it all comes easily."

Robin's happy about the changes on the *Mork* set this year. "They got back to Mork and Mindy—their relationship—Mindy's family. I think everyone realized that's what was missing in the show last season. There were too many outside characters that Mork and Mindy were helping, when the audience apparently wants to see them helping each other."

Robin's probably right, because millions of people love the characters he and Pam Dawber have made household words. They want to learn and grow with both of them, and this season it looks as if the viewers are going to get the chance.

LARRY WILCOX
(Officer John Baker on CHiPS)

Working on a hit series like NBC-TV's *CHiPS* often means putting in a twelve-hour work day for Larry Wilcox. But he's not complaining.

"Sometimes I arrive on the set at seven o'clock in the morning and I'm still there at eight o'clock that night," he says, "but I can take it because it's an easy show to do. As an actor there is not a lot of demand on your talents, although it's a great experience and I'm making a good salary."

Another thing Larry likes about the show is the fact that there's no violence. "It's entertaining, light, and fast-moving, and most important of all, it shows two policeman who are basically nice people. Cops are often portrayed as tough, un-caring guys, and along come Ponch, my co-star

Erik Estrada's character, and Jon, and they're different because they're really concerned about helping."

The subject of his co-star Erik Estrada is something Larry doesn't like to bring up these days. Over the last year the two have basically gone their own ways when they're not on the set working. "We work together well on the show," Larry reveals, "but we just have different interests and life-styles when we go to our homes at the end of the day."

Larry's life-style today revolves around his wife of several months, Hannie Strasser. "This is definitely not going to be your typical Hollywood marriage," Larry vows. "I love my career, but I love Hannie more."

The two were wed in a small, private ceremony in the ballroom of a small hotel. Bouquets of flowers filled the mirror-lined room, and the couple exchanged rings and red roses.

Together they enjoy sports like snow skiing and jet-skiing, and when Larry has several days off, they hop into their motor home and take off for some outdoor camping. "Although we're not the partying type and tend to stay home together—spending time together in a different location is always wonderful."

A DAY IN THE LIFE
OF JIMMY BAIO

What's it like to be an 18-year-old guy who owns his own home, drives a Mercedes, and stars in a hit television series like *Soap*? "Sure, it's a lot of fun, excitement, and glamor," Jimmy says without hesitation, "but there's also a lot of hard work involved. I don't think many people know how many hours you have to put in to tape a half-hour series. Most kids get up, go to school, come home, fool around until dinner time, do a little homework, watch television or play records, and go to bed."

Here's a sample of what Jimmy's daily schedule is like when he's taping *Soap*.

7:00 A.M.   The alarm clock rings, but Jimmy just turns it off and goes back to sleep. ("At 7:15 my manager calls me on the phone, and he doesn't stop ringing the phone until I answer it. My cousin Scott Baio who's on *Happy Days* has the same problem getting up. Maybe it runs in the family!")

8:00 A.M.   Jimmy's showered and dressed. ("Now I feed my dog Jasmine, make my bed, hang up the clothes I dropped on the floor the night before, and sit down to a cup of tea and the newspaper.")

8:30 A.M.   He looks over his script one more time. Since it's Thursday, there will be a complete dress rehearsal today. (Jimmy's weekly schedule goes something like this: Monday—the

70

cast reads the week's script for the first time. They never know in advance what will be happening to their characters that week. Tuesday and Wednesday are all-day rehearsals, going over lines, finding out where to sit or stand. Thursday is dress rehearsal, and blocking—that's film terminology for camera angles. Will they shoot from the back, the side, do a closeup? It all must be decided and Friday is taping day, but more on that later.)

9:30 A.M.   Jimmy locks up his house, says goodbye to Jasmine one more time, and heads to the Sunset/Gower Studios where *Soap* has its headquarters.

10:00 A.M. Jimmy arrives at wardrobe and makeup.

10:30 A.M. He says good morning to the cast and crew and work begins. Until 1:00 everyone rehearses, then a lunch break is called.

2:00 P.M.   Back from lunch and more runthroughs until 6:00 or 7:00 P.M.

7:15 P.M.   Jimmy changes out of his "Billy Tate" outfit and into his own clothes.

8:00 P.M.   He pulls up at home and is greeted with happy barking from Jasmine.

9:00 P.M.   Jimmy's relaxed a bit and ready to eat something light for dinner. ("Since I get home so late I don't like to eat anything heavy. Usually I eat a very big lunch instead.'')

10:00 P.M. Jimmy watches a little TV, reads one of his favorite books, or works on a project around the house. Sometimes he'll practice his karate to keep in shape.

11:30 P.M. Jimmy tumbles into bed—so he'll be able to have a good day tomorrow.

Out of all the working days, Jimmy admits his favorite is Friday. ''Taping before a live audience is wonderful. When they laugh and have a good time it makes everything seem worthwhile.''

On Fridays the day doesn't start until 1:00 P.M., because it usually runs close to 10:30 P.M.! From 1:00 until 2:30 there's a final run-through, then everyone takes a lunch break from 2:30 until 3:30, and then they head for makeup and wardrobe.

''The first taping begins at 4:30,'' Jimmy explains. ''We do two complete tapings in front of two separate audiences, then the film editors take the best parts of each and put them together to make the complete show!''

Doing the two shows (the second is at 7:30) usually lasts until 9:00 P.M., but after the audience leaves the set, there's still more work to be done!

''Now the camera does closeups on each person, and we have to say over any lines that might have been drowned out by audience laughter. Sometimes it takes until 10:00, but sometimes we run as late as midnight!''

Finally, when everything is completed to the

director's satisfaction, the entire cast heads wearily to Martoni's, an Italian restaurant not far from the studio. "We all sit around a couple of hours, relaxing and eating. They've got wonderful pasta. I usually order fettucini."

As you can see, Jimmy's weekdays are very busy, but he does get to relax once in a while. Taping on *Soap* usually takes place from mid-July until mid-March, and then Jimmy's free for four months. Of course, during this time he likes to go back to New York to visit his family, or look for other film projects to do.

On weekends he often heads for Palm Springs, where he enjoys playing tennis and golf and just basking in the sun and swimming. "I love playing softball too, and often the cast will get together at a park and have a game. Sometimes we'll play against other shows, like the *Happy Days* cast or the *Taxi* gang. It's a lot of fun, and fans gather around and have a good time watching, cheering us on. When it's over, we sign autographs or talk to fans who come up and have questions."

Another favorite pastime for Jimmy is auto racing, and sometimes he'll head to the Malibu grand prix to do a little driving himself. "I'm real careful. I wear a helmet and follow all the rules," he assures us. "I'm very big on safety!"

Everyone's glad about that. After all, Jimmy's got a promising career ahead of him—filled with many busy and rewarding days.

ALISON ARNGRIM:
NASTY NELLIE'S NATURALLY NICE
(Offscreen, That Is!)

On stage, on *Little House on the Prairie*, Alison Arngrim isn't very nice. She teases people, plays pranks, speaks harsh words, and really lives up to her name, Nasty Nellie Oleson.

But off the screen, Alison is one of Hollywood's most popular young ladies, and everyone says she's a charming, sweet, and talented star.

You might think that Alison's goal in life (and she has achieved this!) is to be a successful actress, but do you know what she enjoys just as much? Performing stand-up comedy! That's right! When Alison gets home from the set at night, she doesn't relax, or go to bed early, or spend time with one of her many hobbies (she raises boa constrictors—snakes!, loves to read and cook). She jumps in the shower, changes, and heads to The Improvisation or the Comedy Store or the Bla Bla Cafe, where she does a comedy routine!

"I became interested in comedy about three years ago. I was sitting in a comedy club one evening watching a comedian, and I started heckling him from the audience. He'd make jokes back and the audience was laughing. I thought to myself, 'Hey, I'd like to be up there making jokes,' so a few weeks later, I wrote some material and performed it at one of the clubs in Hollywood where they have talent night for amateurs. Boy, was I scared. But when I got up there and started, and saw the audience liked me, I forgot all about being afraid!"

Now, 18-year-old Alison does her popular comedy routines at least once a week in Southern

California, and when *Little House* is on hiatus, she does them all over the country. One of her best-loved routines is her impressions of Amy Carter.

For the last several months, Alison has been living in her own condominium in West Hollywood. But she says she's not really into buying things. In fact, she still drives her 1957 pickup truck. "It gets good mileage and I love it," she sighs.

Alison needs good mileage too, because often it takes her an hour to get to work when the cast is shooting on location in Simi Valley. That's generally one day a week, and the other four days are spent filming at MGM Studios in Culver City, about 25 minutes from Alison's home.

"I start my day with a super-dose of vitamins, some juice, milk, and a muffin or cereal, and then I'm off. For lunch I'll have a salad, and for dinner I like to experiment in the kitchen when I've got time, which isn't often."

Alison's not kidding when she says that, either. She usually works Monday through Friday from 7:00 A.M. until 7:00 P.M. filming, and often her lunch hour is filled with interviews or photo sessions. "I've got a lot of energy, though," she smiles, tossing her long, blond hair from her face. "I love to go, go, go!"

For her role as Nellie, Alison has to spend at least one hour a day in makeup and hair styling. "A lot of people don't know that I wear a wig on the show! It would take too long to fix my hair that way everyday, so they simply pin a wig on me. It takes a lot of pinning to get it in place to last all day, and I've got separate wigs for each style Nellie wears. It might be easier than working with my own hair, but boy does it get hot under that thing, and it's very uncomfortable to wear all day."

Still, Alison is a professional and feels it's just part of her job. One thing that's not *just* part of her job is her friendship with Melissa Gilbert. "Over the years we've become best of friends, and we do things together on the weekend. I tease her a lot because she still has to go to school on the set, while I've graduated. But then she turns around and teases me, because since I'm eighteen now, I have to work as many hours as they want me to. Melissa's sixteen and she's not allowed to work more than eight hours each day. Sometimes when her eight hours are up, she'll say something like, 'Gee, too bad you've got to work late. I was thinking of going to a movie, or a rock concert!'"

That really gets Alison because those are two of her favorite things. "On the weekends I love to go to concerts—I'm really into New Wave Punk, but sometimes good groups play at spots in Hollywood during the week, and if I'm working I can't go."

But then, being the professional she is, Alison shrugs. "Well, that's show biz!"

BENSON BUDDIES: GUILLAUME AND GOLD

When Benson puts his arm around little Katie, and looks into her eyes, or reassuringly pats her on the back when something's troubling her, you just know everything is going to turn out fine, right?

That's because the special look given by Robert Guillaume, who stars as the witty, sarcastic, yet caring, butler on *Benson*, comes straight from his heart.

"When I first started on the series," says 10-year-old Melissa Gold, "it was the first time I had to work in front of a live audience. I was scared. I tried to concentrate on my role, but I was different from myself in front of all those people. I felt like everyone was watching me!"

"Well, they were," laughs Robert. "We were taping in front of a live audience. She didn't do badly at all. In fact, I think she's a heartbreakingly good little actress."

Melissa, whose friends and family all call her Missy, admits that having Robert around that first time really helped. "He talked to me, laughed with me, tried to make me forget about the audience, and after a while it wasn't hard at all. In fact, it was fun, and the audience seems to have such a good time. That's important to the actors."

Missy lives just outside of Los Angeles with her sister Tracey, who is a year older, her mother and father, and toddler sister Bonnie. Like Missy, Tracey is also an actress and starred in last season's *Shirley*, and in *Roots*.

Blond-haired, blue-eyed Missy loves animals

but says, "Right now all I've got time to take care of is my hamster named Benson." She works on the set five days a week and has a private tutor for her schooling requirements.

"I really love acting, but I want to go to college and be a scientist. I'd like to invent watermelon juice," she laughs. And, for all her success as an actress, she is still shy, especially when recognized on the street.

Part of the appeal of the series is the relationship Robert Guillaume has with all the characters on the show. He's snide with Miss Kraus (played by Inga Swenson) and with Taylor, the Governor's assistant played by Lewis J. Stadlen; often fatherly with the Governor (James Noble) as well as Katie; and confiding and genuinely friendly with the Governor's secretary Marcy, played by Caroline McWilliams.

"I think we've got a great cast," smiles Robert, and he's serious. "We're a hit, and it's everyone working together who's responsible."

The *Benson* cast is a warm, close one, and often at lunch breaks Robert will head with Missy to get a bite to eat. "She's professional, loving, and outgoing with people she knows," he says about his little co-star. "She's the kind of girl who isn't afraid to tell you what she's really feeling inside, as long as she knows you'll take her words seriously and knows you do care about her feelings, though she's just a kid."

If Robert's affection for Missy is apparent when you talk to him or see him with her on and off the set, Missy's feelings for him are just as evident. During breaks in rehearsals she'll sit by his side, ask him questions, tell jokes, or play games with him. "I've learned a lot from him too," she smiles. What Missy especially likes is the fact that Robert doesn't just hang around her because they work together. He genuinely loves youngsters.

Off the set, a lot of Benson remains in Robert. He's got the same witty personality, can often be sarcastic, and is very good with comebacks. But like Benson, he's got a heart of gold, and friends find him warm, friendly, and outgoing.

He loves entertaining at home, and that always includes playing the piano and singing for his guests and friends. He's very close with his two sons (now in their 20's) from a marriage that ended in divorce, and he enjoys spending time with them.

Robert's success on *Benson* has opened many doors for him, among them movies and the chance to sing in Las Vegas. His first movie will be Neil Simon's *It Seems Like Old Times!* Actually, for Robert it doesn't! *These* times are going simply sensationally for him and nobody deserves it more!

LORENZO LAMAS
ON LORENZO LAMAS

Lorenzo Lamas is one good reason to stay home on Saturday nights. And even though his CBS series, *Secrets of Midland Heights,* is on at 10:00 P.M., he's worth staying awake for. Twenty-two-year-old Lorenzo is a very outgoing, outspoken, and confident young man. Let him tell you a little about himself now.

"I was born in Santa Monica, California, on January 20, 1958. My mom's the actress Arlene Dahl and my dad's the actor Fernando Lamas. I'm six feet two inches tall and weigh about one hundred and eighty-five pounds. My hair's brown and so are my eyes.

"When I was ten years old, I had a big crush on Raquel Welch. My dad was starring in a film with her, and they were shooting on location in Spain. It was summertime, so I got to come along. Every night after dinner I'd kiss Miss Welch good night!

"I went to school at the Admiral Farragut Military Academy in Pine Beach, New Jersey. I didn't like it, but that's where my mom sent me when I was thirteen. She's an actress and didn't really have time to raise a kid day by day. At a school like this I lived on campus and just went home for vacations. The first two years weren't too pleasant because I was at the bottom of the totem pole. I had to make the beds of five officers. It got a little better when I became an officer myself. In fact, the last two years there, I was the big man on campus and president of my senior class.

"My parents were divorced when I was a toddler, and though I lived with my mom, I spent every summer with my dad. He was married to Esther Williams, the famous swimmer and actress, and she taught me how to swim almost before I could walk without falling down. I'd crawl to the edge of the pool, jump in, and swim around like a tadpole.

"After I graduated from school in 1975, I came back to California to live with my dad and Esther. I wanted to see how the real world operated. After all, living at a military academy is a very different life-style.

"Six months later I moved to an apartment in Santa Monica. The first night I was there alone, I said, 'Well, this is what you wanted. Now what?' I was scared stiff. I had never thought about paying things like rent or car insurance or buying food. I knew my parents would give me money if I needed it, but it was important for me to feel independent and make it on my own.

"So, I parked cars at McDonald's and showed people how to lift weights at a gym. I was lifting weights every day. It was a boring job, but a good one. I worked from ten A.M. until ten P.M. three days a week and got paid a whole ninety dollars!

"Since I really didn't have any strong motivation leading me anywhere else, the idea of acting began to take hold. I'm very emotional and I like becoming different people. I enjoy the reactions I see in people's faces at a movie and the idea of walking out of a theater and feeling or thinking a little differently because of something you've seen, even if it only lasts five minutes or five hours—that's incredible!

"I enrolled in acting school and did a little TV work and then was offered a small part in *Grease*, the movie starring John Travolta. But I was told I'd have to dye my hair blond for the role—I would have dyed it green for the role!

"After that I got a leading part in *Take Down*, a film about a high school wrestling hero, and then *Promises in the Dark*, and *Tilt* with Brooke Shields.

"Last season I was on *California Fever* with Jimmy McNichol, and this year it's *Secrets of Midland Heights*. I hope this one is a hit, because it's an interesting show and I enjoy working with my co-stars who include Stephen Manley and Linda Grovenor, among others.

"It's true that it was a little easier for me to start a career in acting because my parents were well-known personalities, but once I got through the door I was on my own. In fact, producers often expect more from me because they compare me with my dad.

"I love, love, love dancing. I go out about twice a week to kick up my heels on the dance floor. My other hobbies are surfing, skiing, motorcycling, and karate.

"My favorite things to eat are barbequed chicken and for dessert—lemon meringue pie. I enjoy watching John Travolta and Glynnis O'Conner on the screen, and when I watch TV I usually tune in to *Vegas*, *Mork and Mindy*, or *Saturday Night Live*. (And of course, *Secrets of Midland Heights*—I hope you're watching it, too!)"

CHARLENE TILTON:
She wants to learn it all!

Like some young people, Charlene Tilton, who stars as Lucy Ewing on *Dallas*, wasn't too thrilled about going to school every day. "I didn't think I needed history, algebra, or math, because I was going to be in show business," says the petite, blond-haired girl.

But now that she's an actress starring on one of TV's top-rated shows, Charlene has discovered that education is very important. "I spent most of my high school years being a pom-pom girl, cheerleader, and homecoming queen, and now I've got to learn the things I neglected. I really admire people like Jane Fonda, Barbra Streisand, and my co-star Larry Hagman. They're well-read, traveled, and educated. They can talk about a lot of things and they speak so well."

In fact, Charlene uses Jane Fonda as a role model. "She's great and so well respected because she's no dummy," Charlene says admiringly. "She's where I hope to be someday. She stands up for what she believes in, and the movies she makes get people to take notice, think about things. That's what I'd like to do. Use my career as an instrument to make things happen. I'd like to get out and spread a little knowledge about important issues."

Charlene, who began her professional acting career only a few years ago, was born in San Diego, California, but lived with relatives in Illinois until the age of eight, because her mother was ill. But then the two of them moved to California, and Charlene enrolled in workshops, singing classes, and tap dancing school. Later, she participated in every drama production at Hollywood High School and seemed to have a natural talent for acting.

"I always loved going to movies," she says. "Today I enjoy films with a good message, but there's nothing wrong with fun movies either. I'd like to do both kinds."

Although people call Charlene a "sex symbol" because of her role on *Dallas*, the young actress hopes the part won't typecast her in the future. "In fact, besides acting, I'd love to be a director someday, and a writer as well. I already have my own production company called Happy Expressions, and I'm working on two projects for it."

Charlene feels she's been very lucky with her career so far. "I wish everyone could have the opportunity I've had." Her career actually started during her junior year in high school, when a Japanese production company came to her school looking for a girl to cast in a commercial. "They happened to see me and asked me to do it. I said 'Fine,' " Charlene recalls.

After that she appeared in 15 other commercials and did guest roles on shows like *Happy Days, Eight Is Enough*, and *Policewoman*. Her first film was *Freaky Friday*, for Walt Disney.

Although Charlene doesn't *dislike* her TV character on *Dallas* (who's a little mean), she's interested in playing other roles, like the character she portrayed in a just-completed movie-of-the-week for ABC. "She's the opposite of Lucy, and doing the role gave me a chance to see what I could do with a different type of girl."

But Charlene is loyal to the show that made her name well known in America. "The show has been wonderful for me. I've met so many great people and I've learned so much. I wouldn't mind if the series ran for forty years!"

Tiny Charlene, who's 20 years old, stands just 5 feet tall and weighs about 90 pounds. Her hair measures over two feet long, and it's her pride and joy. When she's not working she loves gymnastics, horseback riding, and water skiing, though she confesses that most of her free-time activity is career-oriented.

THINGS YOU DIDN'T KNOW ABOUT YOUR TV FAVORITES

GARY COLEMAN

The cast of *Diff'rent Strokes* is like one big, happy family, and even when they're not filming, they enjoy hanging out together. Gary and his co-stars enjoy roller skating and love whizzing around on wheels. Although Gary's been living in California for a while now, he still calls Zion, Illinois, his home "and favorite place." In fact, the almost 12-year-old says, "I hate California. You can have the smog and the cars." But since he's here, Gary has opened his own production company called Gary Coleman Productions. "Last year we did *The Kid from Left Field* as our first project, and we're going to be doing more in the future." That's not bad for a kid. What Gary would like to do is something like *The Empire Strikes Back*. "I loved that movie, I was so excited when it was shown last summer and I got to go to a press screening before it was released!"

LONI ANDERSON

"A lot of people who watch *WKRP in Cincinnati* think my character, Jennifer Marlowe, is just a sexy, dumb blond. I don't feel that way," says Loni. "Sure she's sexy, but she's smart too, and always totally in control." If you think Loni's the kind of lady who loves parties and going out—you're right, she does. But she also enjoys spending quiet weekends with her husband, Ross Bickell, and her 16-year-old daughter, Deidra. Loni admits that when she first came to Hollywood about five years ago, she didn't want to star in a series. "I thought I'd just do guest spots or parts in movies. Series take so much time away from your family." Now that she's been with *WKRP* for a couple of years, she's changed her mind. "I love the show, and I always try to make time for the people I love too."

GREG EVIGAN

Greg Evigan, of *B. J. and the Bear*, and his wife Pam are a little different from most Hollywood couples. Often the husband is the wife's manager, but in Greg's case, it's Pam who manages him, at least as far as his career is concerned. "At home we both manage each other," laughs the tall, slender Greg. Greg and his wife share a cozy, cottage-type house in the Hollywood Hills. They enjoy spending Sunday mornings breakfasting on the veranda off the living room, when the weather allows, and in Southern California that's quite often. "Pam's a great cook," says Greg, and she admits he's not so bad himself. To the Evigans, privacy is very important, and they don't like to share their personal lives with everyone who comes along. "When you're in the spotlight as much as I am, you need a corner where nobody is allowed—except the one you love."

CINDY WILLIAMS

The perky, talented star of *Laverne and Shirley* loves being part of her hit series for lots of reasons, but an important one is that the show keeps changing. "When we first started out seven years ago, Laverne and Shirley were just 'bimbos,' the term they used to describe anyone who was kind of a dummy. But over the years the characters have grown, matured, and the scripts have dealt with important things like relationships, death, alcoholism, self-confidence, war. Real problems. It's nice because I feel that even though our show

is a situation comedy and the characters are a little zany, it can leave the audience with a worthwhile message. Something to think about.'' Apparently, the followers of this series like the direction the show's taken, because it keeps coming in at the top!

CHERYL LADD

For the last five years, Charlie's blond angel, Chris, has lived in a cozy, cottage-type, two-story house in Beverly Hills. It's a house she's come to love and feel comfortable with. Her beamed-ceiling kitchen with its red tile floor adds such a touch of warmth that most meals are served there rather than in the formal and elegant dining room. Cheryl's a very good cook. "I love to bake—especially pies," she says. But Cheryl's favorite room in the house is her bedroom. With a fireplace, canopy bed, and cozy chairs, no wonder Cheryl loves to curl up here and study her *Charlie's Angels* script for the next day.

Cheryl and her co-star Jaclyn Smith were very sorry to see Shelly Hack leave the show at the end of last season and wish her all the best with her career. "I guess the chemistry just wasn't there between us. Somehow the audience didn't seem to respond to the three of us together,"

Cheryl sighs. Hopefully the newest angel, Tanya Roberts, will prove to be an added attraction for the show. "I like her a lot," admits Cheryl. "I think it will all work out."

GIL GERARD

"Most actors and actresses are in show business because they like to be in it." says Gil Gerard, TV's Buck Rogers. "No matter how much they complain, they must love it because they get up at four-thirty in the morning to be on the set at five, go on location, fight bugs, mud, rain, sun. It doesn't matter. There's a sense of excitement about it." It's true, and Gil is talking about himself too. "Before I went into acting, I had a job advising the Governor of Arkansas. I didn't have to get up so early, I worked in a comfortable environment. But I was totally unhappy, my life was empty. Today I work long hours and fight those bugs on location, but I love my life." Gil admits he enjoys all aspects of show business. "I like writing, directing, producing, acting, film editing. I love it all, being involved with a good show."

TONY DANZA

After starring on a hit series, *Taxi*, for two years, how does 5'11", brown-haired Tony Danza feel about this season's third year for the show? "I don't think I could ever get tired of it," he confesses. "Everyone gets along so well, we have so much fun together, we even hang out on weekends, or sometimes in the evening." It's true too, for often when Tony Danza is seen about town, he has Marilu Henner or Jeff Conoway with him. Sometimes on Monday nights the cast and even the crew members head for the roller skating rinks. Or if Andy Kaufman, who plays Latka, is doing live comedy at a club in town, Tony and Judd Hirsch will drop by to see his routine. But the biggest event of all happens every Friday night right on the set! After the taping is over and the audience has gone home, everyone gathers in the dressing rooms to let off steam. "We have music, and dancing, we each toast a glass of champagne to another script completed, and hopefully another high-rated show, and we've got mounds of food to eat. In fact," beams Tony, "our *Taxi* party is so popular on the Paramount lot that stars from other shows often drop by when their tapings are complete." It's true too, for an observer could see actors like Robin Williams, Henry Winkler, Penny Marshall, and Scott Baio mixing with the *Taxi* crowd. "It's terrific, and a wonderful way to end a week of hard work," Tony says.

HERE'S BOOMER...
AND EVERYONE'S GLAD

It's about time there was another show on television in which the dog was the star! Not since
Lassie and Rin Tin Tin has a canine come along
who has so captured the hearts of viewers. Even
Benji, who's a star of feature films, isn't on a
weekly television series.

According to Boomer's owner and trainer, Ray
Berwick, his floppy-eared mutt was born in Los
Angeles, somewhere around the spring of 1976.
He's 18″ tall, weighs in at 45 pounds, has a brown-
and cream-colored coat and brown eyes—big,
brown, expressive eyes!

Boomer was rescued from the Los Angeles dog
pound by his trainer, who went there looking for
a dog who had a lot of dignity and class. "I was
looking through a group of cages and there he
was. At first he was suspicious of me," says Ray,
"but eventually he came up to say hello."

The trainer took Boomer home, but his wife
got upset when her poodle and Boomer had a
squabble. (Of course, Boomer was blamed for
starting the whole thing—though he'd deny it if
he could speak.) But Ray told her the dog was
just a kid, having fun fooling around, and Boomer
stayed on to become great pals not only with the
entire family, but with the poodle as well!

"Boomer prefers the company of people to
other animals," says his trainer. "He makes
friends easily. I call him a people dog," to which
Boomer barks his agreement!

Did it take a while for Boomer to learn a lot
of tricks? Not compared to other dogs. He was
a very quick learner and never a quitter. He'd try

and try until he learned the lesson. He is especially good at picking up hand signals—something very important when working on a movie set where no speaking is allowed.

After a few years of training many hours a day, Boomer can talk, lie down, roll over, climb a ladder, go right or left on command, act sick, put his feet up, and put his eyes down and lower his head. He can scratch on cue, sneeze, or even fake a limp, among other things. Now how many dogs on your block can do that?

Besides his starring role in *Here's Boomer*, Boomer has done guest appearances on shows like *Baretta* and *Starsky and Hutch*.

This year's scripts are a little different from last year's for one important reason: Boomer now has a home, and though he continues checking out the neighborhood, changing and enriching the lives of those he meets, he goes home each night to his new master and mistress.

It's reported that Boomer gets along very well with everyone on the set. He doesn't demand a lot of extras like a fancy dressing room or limousine service, just a comfortable bed to rest on, a fresh bowl of water, and a good bone to chew. And that makes him different from a lot of Hollywood stars!

TV CROSSWORD

Put on your thinking cap and have some fun!
(Answers on page 121.)

ACROSS

1. She's the wacky star of *Saturday Night Live*.
5. *Bewitched* witch (first name).
8. Famous TV dog (3 words).
10. Initials of actress who plays Nellie Oleson on *Little House*.
11. TV series about Army life for doctors and nurses.
14. Mork is from this planet.
16. On *Star Trek*, the name of the spaceship is the _ _terprise (fill in the first two letters).
17. Last name of actor who plays Tommy Bradford on *Eight Is Enough*.
18. Name of the shipwrecked boat on *Gilligan's Island*.
20. Name of the actress who plays Officer Bonnie Clark on *CHiPS* (initials only).
21. _____ Fu.
22. When Laverne and Shirley need hope, they sing, "Just what makes that little old _ _ _, try and move that rubber tree plant . . ." (fill in the blanks with a 3-letter word).
24. Comedy about roommates (two girls and one guy).

26. Initials of TV character played by 38 Across.
27. What Miss Kraus on *Benson* says for "Yes" (German).
30. Last name of 2 down.
32. _____ Linden (he's Barney Miller).
33. _____ Lamas of *Secrets of Midland Heights*.
34. Series about three heavenly detectives.
38. Star of *Vegas* (last name)
39. Last name of actress who's Julie McCoy of *Love Boat*.
40. He's Sanford (initials).
41. Valerie Harper played _____ Morgenstern.
43. *Happy Days* character, _____ Cunningham.
44. Sarah _____ of *Real People*.
45. _____ Arnaz (Ricky Ricardo on *I Love Lucy*).
46. Chrissy on *Three's Company* (initials).

DOWN

1. *WKRP in Cincinnati* star (first name).
2. First name of 30 across.
3. He plays 43 across.
4. Last name of mother on *One Day at at Time*.
5. Initials of ex-angel.
6. Initials of a TV network.
7. Characters played by Bonnie Franklin and Lynn Redgrave.
9. Lou Ferrig_ _ (fill in the last two letters; he's the Hulk).

103

12. Last name of 1 down.
13. Larry _ _ _ man of *Dallas* (fill in the first 3 letters).
15. _____ Jackson (also an ex-angel).
16. _____ Scott (Ben on *The Waltons*).
18. Jimmy or Kristy.
19. Initials of actor who plays Mr. Roper.
22½. _ _ _works (what ABC, NBC, and CBS are).
23. _____ Rogers of *House Calls*.
25. _____ Laurel and Oliver Hardy.
28. _____ *in the Family*.
29. _____ *Squares*.
30. Actor/comedian _____ Johnson (used to star on *Laugh-In*).
31. Character on *The Waltons* played by Mary McDonough.
33. _____ O'Grady of *Eight Is Enough*.
34. First name of one of 34 across.
35. Ed _____ (he's Lou Grant).
36. Archie Bunker's wife's first name.
37. TV shows on regularly are also called _____ .
39. _____ Bridges of *Diff'rent Strokes*.
41. _____ Taylor of *$1.98 Beauty Pageant*.
42. *The Love Boat*'s physician is called this.

105

POLLY HOLLIDAY: FUN WITH FLO!

"Sit on it!" said the Fonz. "Dy-no-mite!" exclaimed Jimmy Walker in his role as J.J. on *Good Times*, and all across America people were saying it too. Then along came TV's *Alice*, and Polly Holliday in her role as Florence Jean Castleberry, better known as Flo, shouted out, "Kiss mah grits!" And her phrase became famous overnight!

"But did you know that the line originally started out as 'Kiss mah honeydew'?" asks Polly. "It didn't get any laughs, so someone came up with 'Kiss mah grits,' instead. That one really worked—I guess!"

Polly doesn't really have to guess. Not only was "Kiss mah grits" a hit, but so was the show she co-starred on: *Alice*. In fact, the show and Polly's character were so popular during the last two television seasons, the producers decided to give Polly her own show, called, of course, *Flo*.

"Certainly I was a little sad to be leaving all my friends on *Alice*," admits Polly. "And the last show of the season, when Flo left Mel's Diner to head for Houston, from the way we all carried on you'd have thought it was me leaving in real life, not just Flo in a script."

But then Polly tosses back her head and gives a big friendly smile. "My series now is taped just three sets down from *Alice* on the Warner Brothers Studio lot, so I can visit Linda Lavin and the rest of my friends on that show whenever I want."

You could probably walk right by Polly when she's not in character, and never know you had just passed that famous, sassy waitress Flo. Without her red wig, scarf, and flirting wink, Polly is exactly the opposite of Flo. "Flo loves dancing, having a good time, going out, flirting and carrying on, but I enjoy reading, playing the piano, and I basically have a quiet personality."

In fact, before she became interested in acting, Polly's goals included teaching music. She studied classical piano for many years, and enrolled in college as a music major. "But once I was enrolled at Alabama College, I was bitten by the acting bug," Polly says. "I started hanging around the drama department, and I realized the only reason I had studied the piano was that I felt it was something I was supposed to do!"

Like Flo, Polly comes from the South. She was born in Jasper, Alabama, and still returns home at least once a year to visit her mother and all the people she grew up with.

Polly does admit that a little bit of Flo has rubbed off on her. "For the longest time I wouldn't listen to anything but Mozart," she says. "Now I realize I really like country music."

She also admits she gets a lot of marriage proposals. "Oh, not for me," she exclaims, "but for

Flo. And I get letters from women saying they know Flo is really a decent, kind, and sensitive woman under her gum-snapping, hot-tempered ways. Some people say they wish they had a friend like Flo, and that makes me feel good. It's nice to know someone out there relates to your character, would like to know her as a real person."

Although she's had a very successful career (she was also in the film *All the President's Men*), Polly hasn't changed her life-style. "I still like the simple things. I live in the same apartment in Burbank I've lived in for 10 years, and I rent most of my furniture. I just don't want to be bothered with possessions," the actress states.

And Polly never worries about being recognized on the street. "I can go out in public to shop, or eat, and I don't have to worry about not having my privacy. I just don't look, or act like Flo when I'm offstage," she says. "It's just a part I play, but I love it. I have a lot of fun with Flo!"

What makes tapings of *Flo* especially nice for Polly is that restaurant owners and waitresses who come to watch the show (it's taped before a live audience) often come up afterwards and invite her and the cast to their restaurant. "Some are okay," laughs Polly, "but some are as bad as Mel's Diner always appeared to be!"

THOSE OLDIES BUT GOODIES—CONTINUED

MY THREE SONS. . . .
and DAUGHTER, DAWN LYN

My Three Sons was one of the longest-running television series ever broadcast. The first few years featured Fred MacMurray as a widowed father raising his three sons, played by Tim Considine, Don Grady, and Stanley Livingston. William Frawley was their cook, and you might remember him from his role as Fred on *I Love Lucy*. When he passed away, his character was replaced by William Demarest.

A few years later, Tim Considine decided to leave the show and pursue other interests, and since the show was called *My Three Sons*, Barry Livingston (Stanley's brother) was added to the cast as an adopted boy.

Don Grady grew up and was married on the series to Tina Cole. Fred MacMurray fell in love with a widow who had a tiny daughter of her own. She was a little actress named Dawn Lyn, and her character was called Dodie. In the series, Fred married Beverly Garland and adopted Dodie as his own. Don and Tina's characters had twins . . . and the story continued, finally going off the air in 1972.

But everyone still watches it in reruns—the old fans who remember it tune in again and again to recall "the good old days," and new fans find the shows just as terrific!

Today, Fred MacMurray is retired (and yes, he loves those reruns!) and William Demarest was recently awarded a star with his name on Hollywood's famous sidewalk, the "Walk of Stars."

Tim Considine is a business man. Don Grady

is married now and once in a while makes appearances on television shows. Basically he's interested in music, plays seven instruments, and enjoys performing in small clubs in Southern California. Stanley Livingston is doing theater work all over the country, and brother Barry is a successful script writer. Beverly Garland was recently seen on a *Love Boat* segment!

And what about little Dawn Lyn? Well, Dawn will be 18 years old come January, and you probably already know her brother is actor/singer Leif Garrett. Dawn's in the process of recording a country album (she's a terrific singer—just like her brother), and finished starring in a pilot for mid-season in which she plays a young, streetwise girl in a serious dramatic role. "Sometimes when I watch reruns of *My Three Sons*, it's hard to believe that's me on the screen. I started doing the show when I was six years old, and I never thought I would remember all the details of those filming days. But somehow when I watch the shows every little thing comes back to me."

Dawn and her brother Leif live with their mom Carolyn in the Hollywood Hills, and on days when they're all at home together. . . . "Yes," Dawn says as she rolls her eyes, "we sit down and all watch the reruns together." And doesn't your family do that sometimes too?

TV TEST TIME

If you're like most people, you probably spend several hours a week in front of your television set watching dramas, comedies, talk shows—even old shows. But how good a watcher and listener are you? Do you remember what you see and hear? Now you can find out by taking our TV test on the stars and the shows, past, present, and even future! Just fill in the blank, circle true or false, or select the multiple choice answer. When you're finished you'll find the answers on page 120. But no fair peeking ahead of time. Now Get Ready! Get Set! Go!

1. On *Dallas* the role of _____ is played by Charlene Tilton.
2. True or False: Diane Ladd, newcomer on the *Alice* series, also played the part of the free-and-easy waitress Flo in the movie *Alice Doesn't Live Here Anymore*.
3. The name of the cruise director (played by Lauren Tewes) on *Love Boat* is: a) Ms. Romano; b) Julie McCoy; c) Susie Cole; d) Jamie Somers.
4. True or False: Dick York played the original husband on *Bewitched*.
5. True or False: Kate Jackson will return to *Charlie's Angels* this season.

6. *Misadventures of Sheriff Lobo* takes place in: a) Orly County; b) Los Angeles County; c) San Diego County; d) Bakersfield County.

7. The part of _____ on *Breaking Away* is played by Shaun Cassidy. Jackie Earle Haley plays the role of _____ .

8. *Too Close for Comfort* is about: a) two roommates in New York; b) a father who worries about his two daughters; c) a spaceship from Mars; d) a Los Angeles driving school.

9. Diana Canova of *But I'm a Big Girl Now* was in the series _____ .

10. On *Star Trek*, Mr. Spock was: a) a Martian; b) a Vulcan; c) the doctor; d) the computer.

11. The name of the housekeeper on *The Brady Bunch* was: a) Alice; b) Sally; c) Mary; d) Donna.

12. True or False: *I Love Lucy* star Desi Arnaz played the part of a nightclub owner.

13. Lou Grant is: a) the name of a TV series about a Los Angeles newspaper; b) the name of a character on *Mary Tyler Moore*; c) a role played by Ed Asner; d) none of the above; e) all of the above.

14. In the series *Leave It to Beaver*, Beaver's father worked as: a) a lawyer; b) an accountant; c) a doctor; d) an insurance salesman.

15. What do the following TV station initials stand for? ABC _____ ,
CBS _____ ,
NBC _____ ,
PBS _____ .

16. Which show focuses on interesting people and their unique hobbies: a) *Diff'rent Strokes*; b) *Real People*; c) *Rockford Files*; d) *America*?

17. The name of the butler on *Family Affair* was: a) Benson; b) Mr. French; c) Pike.

18. True or False: *60 Minutes* and *20/20* are TV news-magazine shows.

19. *Little House on the Prairie* star Michael Landon has how many children in real life? _____ .

20. True or False: *Knots Landing* is a spinoff show from *Dallas*.

21. The role of Wonder Woman was played by: a) Lindsay Wagner; b) Lynda Carter; c) Loni Anderson; d) Pamela Sue Martin.

22. True or False: Johnny Carson of *The Tonight Show* will be replaced this season by Mac Davis.

23. David Groh acted as a husband in the TV series _____ .

24. *30 Minutes* is a _____ program for kids.

25. True or False: *The Ponderosa* is the name of the cruise ship on *The Love Boat*.

26. *One Day at a Time* star Pat Harrington plays the role of: a) a janitor; b) building superintendent; c) mailman; d) an advertising agency president.

27. Mel's specialty on *Alice* is: a) liver and onions; b) Texas-style chili; c) Navy bean soup; d) barbequed chicken.
    The name of the diner is _____ .

28. What is the name of the TV series whose star owns a dry cleaning business?
   _____

29. True or False: A "pre-empted" program is one which was permanently canceled.

30. The Tony Awards are given for: a) best Broadway shows; b) best TV series; c) best children's programs; d) best TV movies.

31. *Those Amazing Animals* is a TV series about: a) football players; b) the animal kingdom; c) famous zoos; d) none of the above.

32. True or False: Michael Young is the host of the game show *Make Me Laugh*.

33. Dan Haggerty starred in the series
   _____ .

34. *Dallas* star Larry Hagman played the role of an Air Force officer in the series: a) *I Dream of Jeannie*; b) *Please Don't Eat the Daisies*; c) *My Three Sons*; d) *The FBI*.

35. True or False: *Tic Tac Dough* is a TV show about cooking.

36. True or False: *Mork and Mindy* takes place in Chicago.

37. Sonny Shroyer, who plays a Los Angeles Police Department officer in the series *Enos*, previously was in the series
   _____ (four words).

38. True or False: *Buck Rogers in the 25th Century* is a series about a doctor.

39. To whom does the voice of Charlie on *Charlie's Angels* belong? a) James Garner; b) John Forsythe; c) David Birney; d) Lee Majors.

40. True or False: Maude was Edith Bunker's best friend on *All in the Family*.

41. Bob Newhart on *The Bob Newhart Show* was married to a character named: a) Rita; b) Emily; c) Tish; d) Georgette.

42. True or False: *Waltons* character Mary Ellen has a baby named Jamie.

43. *One Day at a Time* star Mackenzie Phillips is the daughter of John Phillips. What is the name of the singing group he was in for many years? _____

44. True or False: *Eight Is Enough* star Dick Van Patten is married in real life to tennis player Joyce Van Patten.

45. True or False: In the *I Love Lucy* series, Lucy was always trying to get into show business.

46. Which *Waltons* star began the tradition of holding hands while praying before dinner during the series? a) Ralph Waite; b) Richard Thomas; c) Michael Learned; d) the late Will Geer.

47. True or False: The Muppets are both hand and body puppets.

48. What is the name of the comedian who wears a paper bag over his head while performing? a) The Unknown Comic; b) Mr. Comic; c) The Invisible Comic; d) Billy T. West.

49. The names of the Three Stooges were _____, _____, _____.

50. The Regal Beagle is a restaurant in which series? a) *Happy Days*; b) *Three's Company*; c) *Alice*; d) *Flo*.

51. True or False: The character of Flo on *Alice* left the diner for a job in California as a gift shop owner.

52. True or False: Suzanne Somers of *Three's Company* is married to Alan Hammill, who does commercials for Alpha Beta markets.

53. True or False: *One Day at a Time* stars Valerie Bertinelli and Bonnie Franklin both threatened to quit the series unless they each received more money per episode.

54. *The Brady Bunch* is a syndicated TV series about: a) the Brady Flower Shop; b) a husband and wife with six kids; c) a teacher named Mr. Brady and his class.

55. True or False: A week's worth of game shows may be taped in one day.

56. The host of the dance show *American Bandstand* is: a) Don Cornelius; b) Dick Clark; c) Lloyd Thaxton.

57. True or False: *All in the Family* characters Michael and Gloria moved to California from New York.

58. True or False: Much of the background laughter in TV comedies is a recorded "laugh track."

59. Ron Ely, host of *Face the Music*, was once which famous TV character? a) Superman; b) Tarzan; c) Dick Tracy; d) Incredible Hulk.

60. True or False: *M*A*S*H* is a TV series about life in an Army camp.

61. True or False: The voice you hear narrating *That's Hollywood* is none other than *Happy Days'* Tom Bosley.

62. Name two popular TV series of the late 1960s and early '70s in which the characters were based on vampires, bats, and Frankenstein monsters: _____ and _____ .

63. True or False: Jameson Parker played the rotten Brad Vernon on the daytime soap *One Life To Live*.

64. What was another series in which Robert Urich of *Vegas* starred? _____

65. True or False: Bob Wagner and Natalie Wood star in *Hart to Hart*.

66. *Sha Na Na* is a half-hour musical show with songs from the: a) 1950s; b) 1960s; c) Today's Top 10; d) none of these.

67. Leif Garrett and Vince Van Patten starred in what short-lived series over five years ago? _____

68. True or False: Almonzo and Laura are characters from *The Waltons*.

69. Danny DeVito, Judd Hirsch, and Jeff Conoway are all stars of what series? _____

70. Before *Diff'rent Strokes*, Todd Bridges played the character _____ on the series _____ .

71. True or False: On *Laverne and Shirley*, Laverne loves to eat: a) cookies; b) hamburgers; c) scooter pies; d) Crackerjacks.

72. Dr. Banner is a character from: a) *Soap*; b) *The Incredible Hulk*; c) *General Hospital*; d) *Trapper John, M.D.*

73. Before John Schneider became a successful actor on *The Dukes of Hazzard*, he earned a few extra dollars by: a) teaching a tap dancing class; b) doing magic tricks; c) delivering papers; d) phone soliciting.

74. True or False: Cheryl Ladd's real name was Cheryl Stoppelmoor.

75. Linda Grovenor of *Secrets of Midland Heights* starred in a film with Robby Benson called; a) *One on One*; b) *Die Laughing*; c) *Kramer vs. Kramer*; d) *Ode to Billy Joe*.

76. *Too Close for Comfort*'s Ted Knight starred on the *Mary Tyler Moore Show* as _____

77. James Garner and Mariette _____ act together in camera commercials.

1. Lucy Ewing
2. True
3. b
4. True
5. False
6. a
7. Dave, Moocher
8. b
9. *Soap*
10. b
11. a
12. False
13. e
14. b
15. American Broadcasting Company
    Columbia Broadcasting System
    National Broadcasting Company
    Public Broadcasting System
16. b
17. b
18. True
19. 4
20. True
21. b
22. False
23. *Rhoda*
24. news-magazine
25. False
26. b
27. b, Mel's
28. *The Jeffersons*
29. False
30. a
31. b
32. False
33. *Grizzly Adams*
34. a
35. False
36. False
37. *The Dukes of Hazzard*
38. False
39. b
40. False
41. b
42. False
43. The Mamas & Papas
44. True
45. True
46. d
47. True
48. a
49. Manny, Moe, Curly Joe
50. b
51. False
52. True
53. False
54. b

55. True
56. b
57. True
58. True
59. b
60. True
61. True
62. *The Munsters* and *The Addams Family*
63. True
64. *S.W.A.T.*
65. False
66. a
67. *Three for the Road*
68. False
69. *Taxi*
70. Loomis, *Fish*
71. c
72. b
73. b
74. True
75. b
76. Ted Baxter
77. Hartley

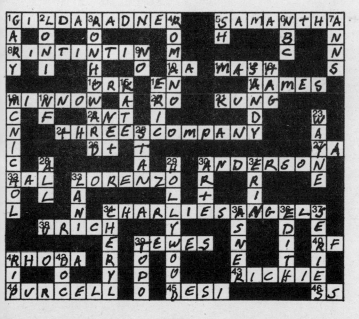